BirdWingFeather

Siri Schillios

Pomegranate Kids

Published by PomegranateKids®, an imprint of
Pomegranate Communications, Inc.
19018 NE Portal Way, Portland OR 97230
800 227 1428 | www.pomegranate.com

Pomegranate Europe Ltd.
Unit 1, Heathcote Business Centre, Hurlbutt Road
Warwick, Warwickshire CV34 6TD, UK
[+44] 0 1926 430111 | sales@pomeurope.co.uk

To learn about new releases and special offers from Pomegranate, please visit
www.pomegranate.com and sign up for our e-mail newsletter. For all other
queries, see "Contact Us" on our home page.

Front cover: **Glow**, 2008, acrylic on wood, 14 x 13.8 cm (5½ x 5⅞ in.)
Back cover: **Snowbird**, 2008, acrylic on wood, 18.4 x 26 cm (7¼ x 10¼ in.)

This product is in compliance with the Consumer Product Safety Improve-
ment Act of 2008 (CPSIA) and any subsequent amendments thereto. A
General Conformity Certificate concerning Pomegranate's compliance with
the CPSIA is available on our website at www.pomegranate.com, or by
request at 800 227 1428. For additional CPSIA-required tracking details,
contact Pomegranate at 800 227 1428.

Library of Congress Control Number: 2013957433

Pomegranate Item No. A234

Designed by Carey Hall

Printed in China

23 22 21 20 19 18 17 16 15 14   10 9 8 7 6 5 4 3 2 1

For Olive and Rolv.
Always and forever, Siri will love you.

SNOWBIRD

IN THE YUM YUM TREE

THE EARLY BIRD

THE BLUEBIRD OF HAPPINESS

GLOW

COAT OF MANY COLORS

FIREBIRD

SMALL WONDER

PARADISE

ENCHANTED EVENING

SWEETNESS AND LIGHT

RED BIRD

Introduction

I like everything about birds. It is a pleasure to hear them sing; they sound so happy, all excited about each new day. Birds add a peaceful and hopeful feeling to the world. Plus, they can fly! And even though I know birds can fly, even though I expect them to, some small part of me is always surprised and delighted when they spread their wings and jump into the air. It is wonderful to see the freedom they have. It lifts my spirits to watch them soar.

Birds have beautiful shapes. I like the way they hold their heads up and puff their chests out. They look so pleased with themselves. Drawing the shape of a bird makes me smile on the inside.

I am a painter who loves to draw, and if you look carefully, you can see the original drawing underneath every one of my paintings. This is why all my paintings have very strong lines.

When I make a painting, I first imagine the whole picture, and then I concentrate on smaller and smaller parts of it. I consider the shape of the whole bird and then the shape of its wings and finally the beautiful colors in each feather. Bird, wing, feather.

My paintings are filled with happy colors. Certain colors are especially excited about getting to sit next to each other in a painting. There are scientific reasons for this, and I have studied them, but I like to think this happens because of a friendship between colors. Green loves to sit next to red, blue feels cozy being around orange, and purple is delighted enough to dance with yellow. People have said my paintings make them feel happy; perhaps this is because I pay close attention to the friendship of colors.

As you turn the pages of this book, I hope you will begin by looking at each whole picture, just the way I did. Can you identify all the colors? On the left-hand page you will see some of the small parts that make up the whole picture shown on the right. All the small parts differ in some way, but each fits perfectly somewhere in the bigger picture. Can you spot the eye and the beak? How about the wing, tail, and feathers? Do you see where each part belongs? What else do you see in the picture? In some of my paintings there are flowers, leaves, or berries. I wonder if you will find the little caterpillar.

Sometimes the birds in my paintings look like real birds—birds I might see in my garden. But I also like to paint imaginary birds of whatever color and shape I can dream up. If you like birds as much as I do, I hope you will try drawing or painting a bird, and that when you do, you will let your imagination fly free.

—Siri Schillios

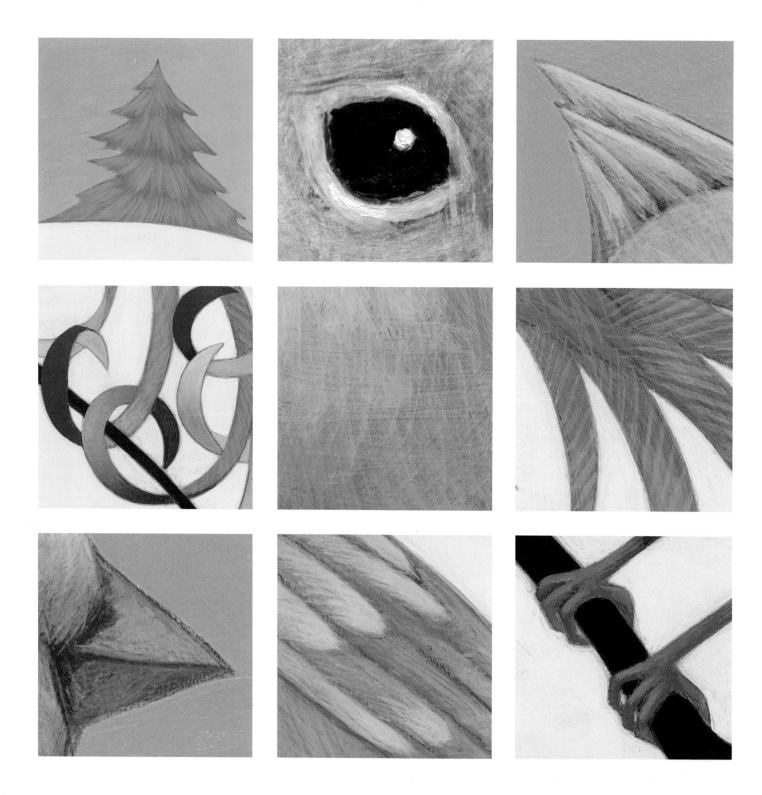

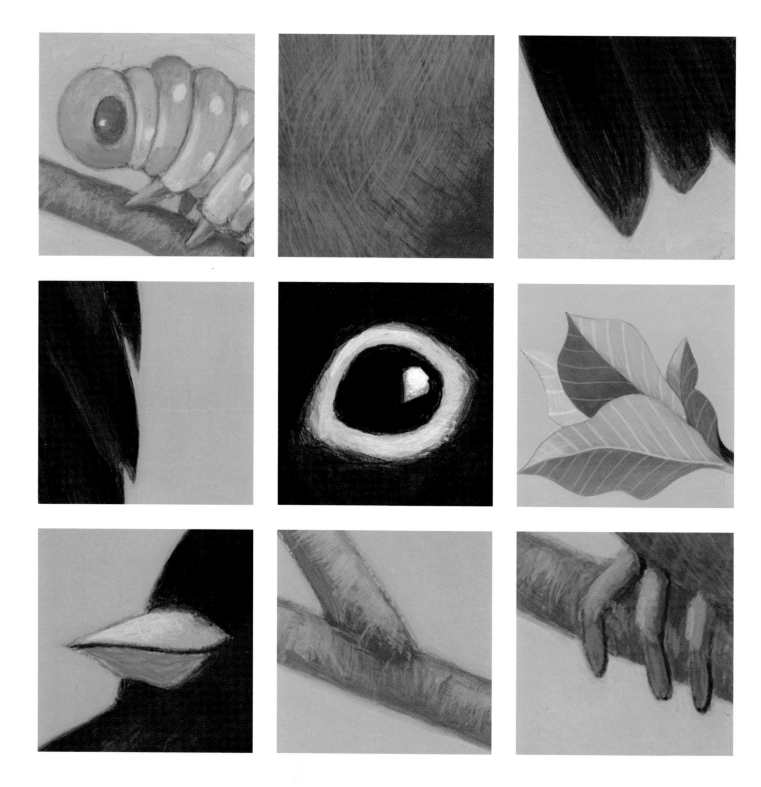

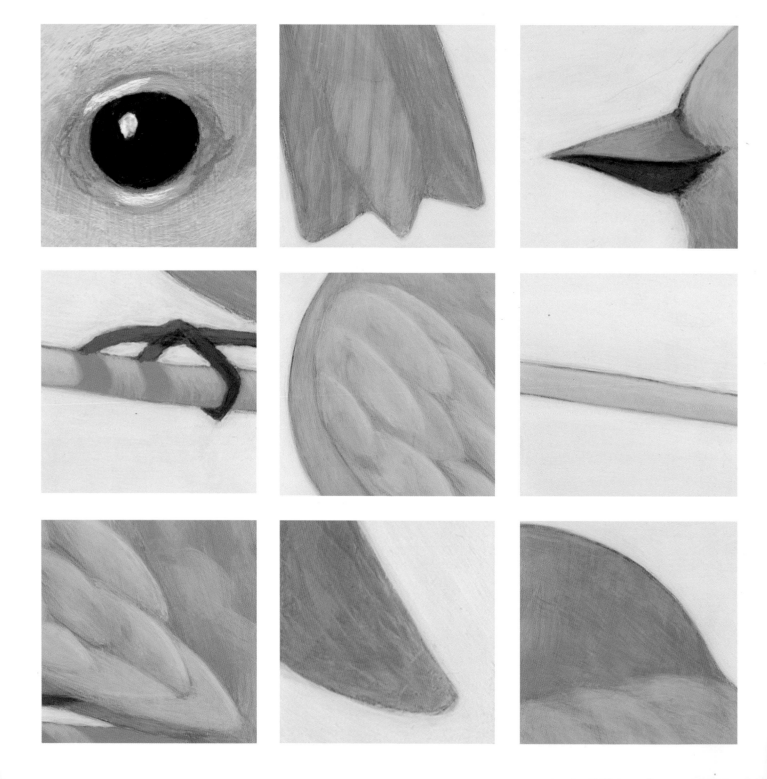

ABOUT THE AUTHOR

Siri Schillios lives in Portland, Oregon, surrounded by an exceptionally colorful garden that has become the happy playground of many birds, a few golden squirrels, and one ancient cat who loves to sleep in the sun.